STEP INTO NATURE

In the Garden

Written by Michael Chinery
Illustrated by John Gosler

GRANADA

Published by Granada Publishing 1984
Granada Publishing Limited
8 Grafton Street, London W1X 3LA

Copyright © Templar Publishing Ltd 1984
Illustrations copyright © Templar Publishing Ltd 1984

British Library Cataloguing in Publication Data
Chinery, Michael
    In the garden. – (Step into Nature; 2)
    1. Gardens – Juvenile literature
    I. Title   II. Series
    712'.6   SB452

    ISBN 0-246-12173-4

Series devised by Richard Carlisle
Edited by Mandy Wood
Designed by Mick McCarthy
Printed in Italy

Contents

No matter where you live, you are surrounded by nature.
In the towns, even in the cities, you will find birds and animals,
plants and trees, and insects to watch and wonder about.
STEP INTO NATURE is about all these things–the everyday
creatures as well as the elusive. It's packed with nature projects
to do, nature diaries to keep and clues and signs for the
nature detective to read. It will teach you how to look at the
world of nature around you, how to understand its working and
how to conserve it for others.

Welcome to the garden!

Most people have a garden of one sort or another outside their house. It might only be very small but within its boundary live a hundred and one different plants and animals. Some may have been put there by the gardener, while others will have made the garden their home quite independently.

Most people grow colourful flowers in their gardens. Many also grow fruit and vegetables to eat. There may be a lawn, a hedge or perhaps an old wall. There might even be a pond. And all of these parts of the garden provide places for wild plants and animals to live. A garden is therefore a very good place to study wildlife, especially birds and insects, and in the following pages you'll find some of the creatures that are probably living outside your house right now.

The cultivated plants in the garden can also be very interesting. You don't usually see them growing in the surrounding countryside, so have you ever wondered where they all came from in the first place? Many did come from the wild originally, but our cultivated flowers and vegetables are generally much bigger than their wild relatives. This is because gardeners have always used seeds from the biggest and best plants. They have done this for hundreds of years, so today's garden flowers are often very different from their wild ancestors. Besides being bigger and brighter, they often have many more petals. In fact, some of them have changed so much that you wouldn't even guess their original form.

Other plants came from warm countries and will only grow here in summer. The runner beans at the back of the picture came all the way from South America!

4

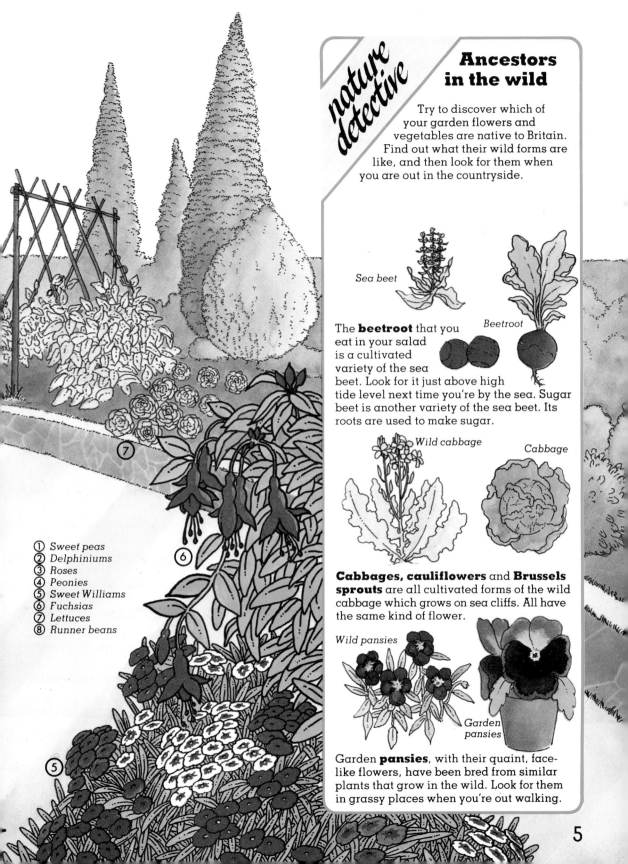

① Sweet peas
② Delphiniums
③ Roses
④ Peonies
⑤ Sweet Williams
⑥ Fuchsias
⑦ Lettuces
⑧ Runner beans
⑦
⑥
⑤

nature detective

Ancestors in the wild

Try to discover which of your garden flowers and vegetables are native to Britain. Find out what their wild forms are like, and then look for them when you are out in the countryside.

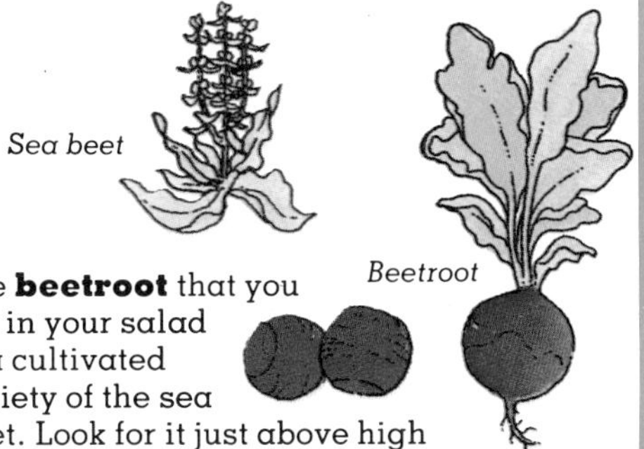
Sea beet
Beetroot

The **beetroot** that you eat in your salad is a cultivated variety of the sea beet. Look for it just above high tide level next time you're by the sea. Sugar beet is another variety of the sea beet. Its roots are used to make sugar.

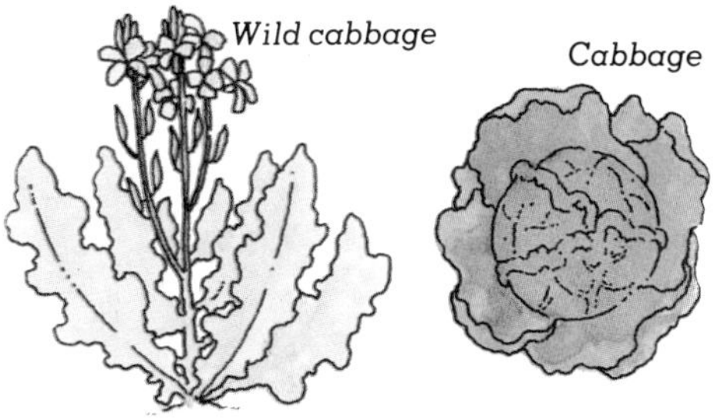
Wild cabbage
Cabbage

Cabbages, cauliflowers and **Brussels sprouts** are all cultivated forms of the wild cabbage which grows on sea cliffs. All have the same kind of flower.

Wild pansies
Garden pansies

Garden **pansies**, with their quaint, face-like flowers, have been bred from similar plants that grow in the wild. Look for them in grassy places when you're out walking.

Bees and flowers

Some of the earliest insects to appear in the garden in spring are the big furry bumble bees. They are all queens which have slept through the long winter. Once awake, they work hard to gather nectar and pollen from the crocuses and other flowers. Have a close look at one of these bees next time you see one in the garden. It won't hurt you, for it is far too busy collecting food. As the long tongue sucks up the flowers' nectar, the bee's furry body picks up lots of pollen dust. Watch carefully, and you might even see the bee comb the pollen off and pack it into the pollen baskets on its hind legs. You can see one of these baskets bulging with yellow pollen in the big picture.

The bee has to visit many flowers to fill its pollen baskets. And while doing this it does a most important job for us in the garden: it pollinates our flowers by carrying pollen from one bloom to another. Until they are pollinated in this way, the flowers cannot produce fruit or seeds. So without bees, we would have no apples or other fruits.

When its baskets are fully loaded, the bee flies back to its nest. This may be under the ground or among dense grass on the surface. A queen will start a nest in the spring and rear a few youngsters, which she feeds on nectar and pollen. They quickly grow into worker bees and set about expanding the nest. They rear many more workers during the summer and carry on pollinating the flowers.

There are several different kinds of bumble bees. Most are black and yellow, but some are brown and some are black with red tails. The honey bee, seen at the top of the picture, is much smaller than the bumble bee but it pollinates flowers in the same way.

6

Bee look-alikes

Many insects, apart from bees, visit flowers to feed on pollen and nectar. Some of them, especially certain flies, are easily confused with bees, although bees have four wings and flies have only two. These bee look-alikes are harmless but birds leave them alone because they look like the stinging bees.

The **drone-fly** belongs to the hover-fly family. It looks very much like a honey bee, but it has much smaller feelers. If you disturb it, it will dart rapidly away and then hover – something that the bee cannot do.

The **bee-fly** has a furry coat and looks very much like a small, brown bumble bee, apart from its wings which look very different. It uses its long tongue to suck nectar from the flowers, but it cannot fold it up like the bee can. The bee-fly can hover like the drone-fly, giving out a high-pitched whine as it does so.

7

Nesting in the garden

Our feathered friends the blue tits and great tits are common visitors to the garden. But they will nest there only if they can find suitable holes in trees or walls. You can encourage these pretty birds to nest in your garden, though, by simply putting up a nestbox. You can always buy one from a pet shop, but it is much more fun to make the box yourself.

Get the box into position well before the nesting season. It should be at least 2 metres above the ground, and preferably fixed to a tree. If you screw it to the tree, rather than nail it, you can take it down more easily for cleaning. If you haven't got a suitable tree handy, then you can fix the box to a wall, but make sure that it is never in the full sun.

The birds will soon start to investigate the box, and if you see them carrying in bits of grass and moss you will know that they are starting to make their nest. *Never disturb them:* the lid of the nestbox is hinged so that you can clean it out in the winter, not so that you can keep looking in at the nest! Instead, watch from a distance with binoculars. When you see the parents both bringing beakfuls of caterpillars to the box you will know that the eggs have hatched. The babies will leave the nest after two or three weeks and you might even be lucky enough to watch their first flying lesson.

Back   Base   Lid   Front

nature project

Making a nestbox

You can make a good nest box from a single plank of wood. Cut it up as shown on the right, and fix the pieces together to make the box shown in the big picture.

What you will need
- A plank of wood 15 cm wide and about 18 mm thick. It does not need to be smooth.
- A drill to make the entrance hole.

Spot the difference

In this panel you can see two kinds of tits which commonly visit the garden. Can you spot the difference between them and the blue tit, shown in the big picture? If you see any of these birds in your garden, make a note of them in your *Nature Notebook*.

The **great tit** (*above*) is much bigger than the blue tit. It has a black and white head and a black stripe down its breast. This stripe is wider in the male than in the female. Like all the tits, it collects lots of small caterpillars for it young.

The **coal tit** (*left*) is about as big as the blue tit but it has a black head and little yellow on its breast. It is best identified by the white patch at the back of its head.

You can make a hinge from an old piece of leather or a strip of rubber cut from an old wellington boot. Simply tack half of the hinge onto the lid of the box and fix the other half to the back of the box. For a neater job, you could ask someone to plane the back of the lid for you so that it fits tightly against the back of the box. You may need help with drilling the hole in the front as well. This should be no more than 28 mm across if you want to encourage blue tits to use the box. If the hole is any larger then house sparrows are likely to build in it before the blue tits are ready to nest.

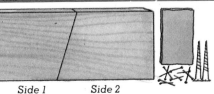

Side 1   *Side 2*

● A hammer, some nails and two strong screws to fix the box to a tree.
● A strip of leather or rubber for the hinge. Tough plastic is also suitable.

9

The earthworm's world

Have you ever taken a really close look at the earthworms that are uncovered every time anyone digs in your garden? There are thousands of them even in the smallest plot and they are very important for the gardener and his plants.

A worm's body is made up of many little rings, called *segments*. You will not be able to see an obvious head, but if you look closely you'll notice that the worm's front end is more pointed than its hind end. The worm has no use for eyes because it spends almost all of its time tunnelling through the soil in the damp and dark. Neither does it need legs. Instead it has tiny bristles on the underside of each segment which it uses to help push its body between the soil particles.

The worm also swallows a lot of soil as it tunnels along. It digests any decaying roots or other matter that it finds and then passes out the remains as worm casts on or near the surface. In fact, the earthworm acts rather like a plough – mixing up the earth and bringing rich soil to the surface. The worm's tunnels help to drain the ground and allow air to reach the plant roots. And on damp nights worms often drag dead leaves down into their burrows which help to enrich the soil. All these activities help the gardener's plants to grow big and strong, which is why worms are such useful creatures to have around!

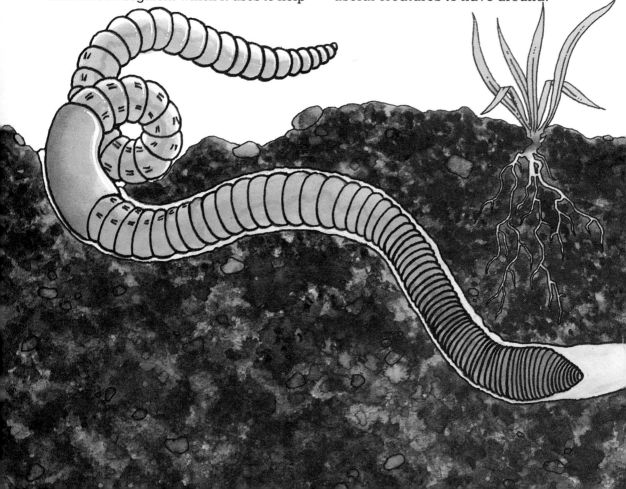

Having worms to stay

You obviously can't see the burrowing activities of earthworms in the wild, but you can watch them at work if you keep some in a special cage called a *wormery*. You can make one yourself, perhaps with a little grown-up help, or you can buy one from a dealer in naturalists' equipment.

Dig up some worms from your garden. But before you put them in your wormery take a close look at their bodies. Can you see the difference between their front and rear ends? Rub your finger gently along the underside of the worm from the back to the front. Can you feel the bristles shown in the big picture? They are only tiny, but next time you see a bird trying to pull a worm out of the lawn you will see just how firmly they anchor the worm in the ground.

1 You can make a simple wormery like the one on the right using two sheets of perspex about 30cm wide and 20cm high, and a strip of wood about 25mm wide and 18mm thick. Cut the wood into three lengths and nail or screw the pieces together to make a wooden frame as shown in the picture. Then screw a sheet of perspex on to each side of the frame. If you are a good carpenter, you might prefer to cut grooves in the frame and slot the sheets in. If you do this, you can use glass instead of perspex.

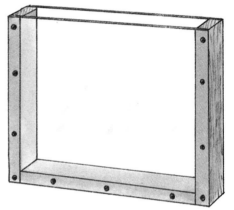

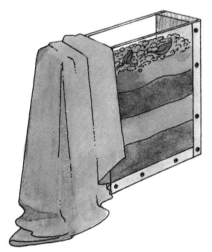

2 Fill your wormery with layers of different types of soil. You can use ordinary garden soil, sand, peat or potting compost, and chalky soil if you can get it. Water the soil well. (It is a good idea to keep your wormery on a waterproof tray, because you will have to water it from time to time.) Then put about half a dozen fairly large worms on the top of the earth and watch them tunnel down into their new home. Scatter a few dead leaves or some grass cuttings on the surface and then cover your wormery with a cloth.

3 Look at the wormery every day, and you will soon see how the worms churn up the soil and mix the layers together. You will probably see some worms moving along by the perspex. Watch how they anchor their hind end and push the front end forward, then anchor the front and pull the hind end along. Remember to add leaves or grass cuttings to the wormery from time to time as food. And don't leave the wormery uncovered for long, because sunlight is harmful to worms. Finally, remember to release the animals when you have finished watching them.

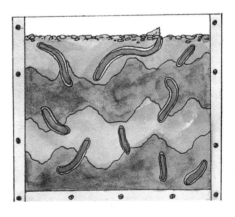

The friendly robin

The robin is a bold and friendly bird and is never far away when the garden is being dug in the winter or spring. As soon as the gardener turns his back, the robin will dash up to perch on the fork handle. It is really searching for worms and other small animals, and sitting on the fork gives it a good all-round view of the freshly-dug earth. If you are very patient you might even get a robin to feed from your hand. Buy it some meal worms from the pet shop, for these are among its favourite foods.

A curious thing about robins is that, although they are friendly towards people, they are certainly not friendly towards other robins. In fact, it's very rare to see two robins together except in the breeding season. Early in the autumn each robin sets up its own territory and sings loudly to warn other robins to keep away. Then, at about Christmas-time, the females leave their own territories and roam through those of the neighbouring males. The males chase them out at first, but the females keep coming back and singing to the males until, eventually, one female is allowed to stay. The birds pair up and, by March or April, the mother bird will have built a nest and in it have laid her white, speckly eggs.

You can encourage robins to nest in a thick hedge or in ivy on a wall by putting up a nestbox like the one on page 8. But for robins don't put the front on. When the young robins emerge you'll notice that they are brown and speckly (like the one on the left) and quite unlike their parents. They will not get their red breasts till late in summer.

nature detective

Colourful birds

The robin is very easy to recognise, but it is not the only bird with a reddish breast. The bullfinch and the chaffinch, which you can see on the right, are both common in gardens. They have much stouter beaks than the robin, showing that they eat different foods. Try to find out what the bullfinch and the chaffinch eat. Why is the bullfinch a nuisance in orchards? Can you spot any other differences between the robin and these two birds?

The robin's territory

Like most male birds, the male robin defends his territory fiercely during the breeding season. The territory may cover several gardens, and if a strange male enters it, the resident robin will attack him. You can sometimes fool your robin into attacking a simple model.

1 Make a model robin using modelling clay. It need not be a very good model, as long as it has a red breast, for this is what makes your robin take notice of the stranger.

2 Fix the model in your robin's territory, making sure that the red breast is clearly visible. Go indoors and watch what happens.

3 When your real robin sees the intruder he will probably sing loudly, and when this has no effect he will attack the model with his beak and claws. But he will soon realise that it is a harmless model and leave it alone. Some robins will even attack nothing more than a bunch of red feathers.

The male **bullfinch** *(right)* has a bright red breast and glossy black cap. The female has a dirty pink breast. You will normally see the male and female together in your garden.

The male **chaffinch** *(left)* has a blue head in the breeding season and a pinky red breast. The female is mostly brown and grey, but she has the same wing pattern.

The slow-moving snail

The best time to watch snails in action is during a warm spring or summer night, especially after a shower of rain. You can also see them after daytime showers, but the snails will not come out if it is dry. This is because their soft bodies dry up very easily in this sort of weather. To prevent this the snails pull their bodies right back into their shells and seal up the openings with a parchment-like cover. They do the same thing in the winter, and usually hide away under stones or rubbish until the warmer weather arrives.

Snails have no legs and they move by gliding slowly forward on the flat part of their body known as the *foot*. If you put a snail in a jam jar and watch it through the glass you will be able to see the rippling movements of the muscles on the underside of this foot. A gland under the snail's head produces a layer of slime which helps the snail to move along more easily. You can see the slime long after the snail has passed, for it dries to form a silvery trail. The snail finds its way largely by smell and touch, picking up signals with its two pairs of tentacles. These will be quickly withdrawn if you touch them with your

finger because they are very sensitive. Right at the tip of the longest tentacles are the snail's eyes but they are not very efficient so the snail doesn't rely on them like we humans do.

The commonest snail in the garden is the one you can see here. It is actually called the garden snail. It is a vegetarian and often destroys our garden plants, especially seedlings. Its mouth, which is underneath its head, has a tongue like a strip of sandpaper which scrapes food from the plants. You can see the mouth when your snail is in the jam jar.

The song thrush loves to eat snails. It hammers the shells on a stone until they break. Look for piles of broken shells in your garden to tell you where the thrush has been eating its dinner.

Night journeys

Have you ever wondered how far a snail travels in its search for food? You can get some idea from this simple project. You can also find out if the snail comes back to the same place to sleep every day.

1 Find some snails in their sleeping quarters in the daytime. Look in thick clumps of plants and in upturned flower pots.

2 Mark some of the snails with a spot of paint. Don't use anything too bright, or birds will find your snails too easily.

3 Go out into your garden with a torch at night and see if you can find any of your marked snails. How far have they travelled from their sleeping quarters?

4 Go back to the snail's sleeping quarters the next morning and look for the marked snails. You will probably find that most of them have returned.

Prickly hedgehogs

If you hear squeals and grunts coming from your garden on a summer night, it may indicate the presence of hedgehogs. Go out with a torch and see if you can find them. The animals don't mind the light too much, but walk quietly if you want to see them properly. They roam the garden soon after dusk in search of slugs, worms and other small animals, and they also like fallen fruit. They make a lot of noise as they shuffle through the flower beds or along the bottom of the hedge. And they can move surprisingly fast on their short legs. You might even find their footprints in the soft soil the next morning. You can see what they look like from the drawing below.

The hedgehog's prickles are really special hairs. They cover the animal's back and sides and give it plenty of protection. When the animal is frightened it rolls itself into a ball, as you can see on the left of the picture. The sharp spines all point outwards to protect the hedgehog's soft underside. Baby hedgehogs have very soft spines at first, but they harden up in just a few days and after about two weeks the babies learn to roll into a ball like their parents.

Hedgehogs always go to sleep in the daytime. They make their beds in the bottoms of hedges or under sheds or piles of rubbish. They also go to sleep for most of the winter, although they may get up to wander about if the weather is mild. This long winter sleep is called *hibernation* and the hedgehog will make a special nest of leaves and grass, perhaps in an old shed, in which to rest until the spring.

nature project

Invite a hedgehog to dinner

Hedgehogs are good animals to have in the garden because they eat up a lot of the troublesome slugs that eat away many garden plants. If you have hedgehogs in your garden, you can encourage them to come every evening by putting out some food. In fact, this might attract them even if they don't normally visit you. They will quickly get used to you if you put the food out regularly, and you will be able to watch them from close quarters. If you're lucky, a female may even bring her babies to feed when they are old enough.

Put the food on an old plate. It should be big enough for more than one hedgehog to feed from it. You can try all kinds of food. Breakfast cereals, hard-boiled eggs, fruit and left-overs from your own dinner will all be gladly eaten. Pet food is also very good, and for a real treat you can give your hedgehog a dish of bread and milk or some raw minced meat, but don't give bread and milk every day.

The industrious ants

A good way to find out if you have ants in your garden is to leave some sweet food, such as half an orange or a piece of melon, lying around outside. If there are any ants around they will soon swarm all over the food, biting pieces out and carrying them back to their nest. Watch them closely and you'll see how they carry pieces of food much larger than themselves, and how they keep coming back until the food has nearly all gone.

Two kinds of ant are common in the garden. One is the black ant, which often nests under concrete paths and under the walls of buildings. The other one is a red ant, which generally nests under stones in the soil, especially in rockeries. Its nests are much smaller than those of the black ant and, unlike the black, it can sting.

All ants live in colonies which are ruled by one or more females called *queens*. The queens are bigger than all the other ants and lay all the eggs. The other ants are nearly all workers and there may be as many as 5,000 of them in just one nest. They spend their time working together to build the nest, to find and collect food, and to rear the younger ants. Apart from being bigger, queen ants are also different from workers because they have wings. They only have them for a short time, though – just long enough for them to fly away from the nest to mate. After this, they break them off and never fly again.

If you watch a line of ants moving to and from some food you will notice that they often stop and rub their feelers together, like those in the big picture. This is the ants' way of "talking" to each other and passing on messages about food that they've found.

Ants eat all sorts of things, including seeds and small insects, but they are especially fond of sweet things. The honeydew given out by greenfly (see page 26) is one of their favourite foods and you can often see ants running over plants to collect it. In fact, greenfly are sometimes known as *ant cows* because some ants actually look after the greenfly and "milk" the honeydew from them, just like we milk real cows.

nature watch

Ants in the air

Every year in July or August, people report seeing great swarms of flying black ants. Both males and females pour out from under stones and through cracks in pavements and take to the air, for this is the ants' mating flight. Swallows and other birds eat huge numbers of these insects but every year enough ants survive to mate and carry on the species. The males die soon after mating, but the females break off their wings and go in search of a new place to start a nest.

Make a note of the weather conditions if you see an ant swarm. The weather controls the ants' activity, ensuring that all the nests in one area produce swarms at the same time.

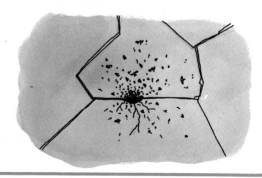

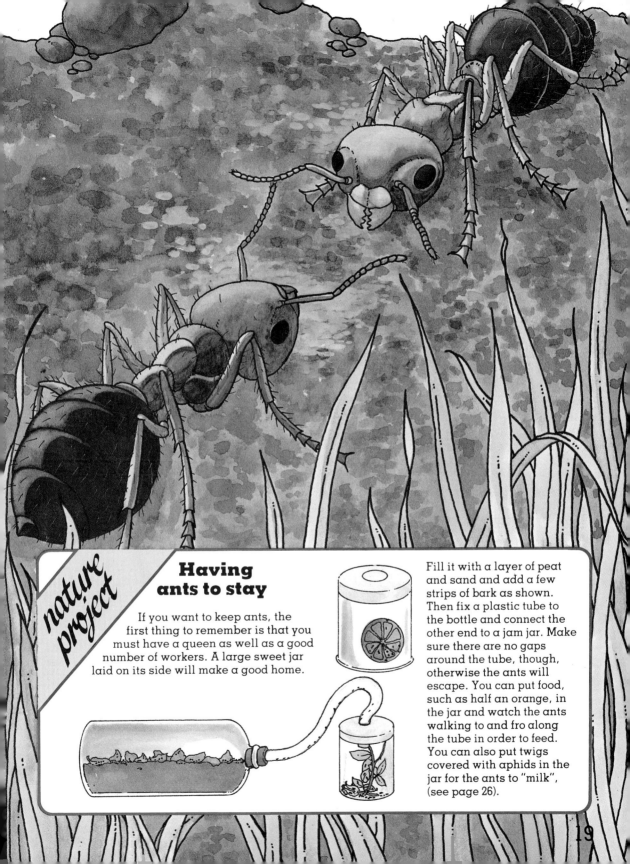

Having ants to stay

If you want to keep ants, the first thing to remember is that you must have a queen as well as a good number of workers. A large sweet jar laid on its side will make a good home.

Fill it with a layer of peat and sand and add a few strips of bark as shown. Then fix a plastic tube to the bottle and connect the other end to a jam jar. Make sure there are no gaps around the tube, though, otherwise the ants will escape. You can put food, such as half an orange, in the jar and watch the ants walking to and fro along the tube in order to feed. You can also put twigs covered with aphids in the jar for the ants to "milk", (see page 26).

Fruits of the garden

Some of the commoner kinds of garden fruits are shown on this page. Can you think of any more? They nearly all grow on trees or bushes, but they cannot start to grow until the flowers have been pollinated by bees or other insects. You can read more about this on page 6. Our garden fruits generally have sweet, juicy flesh and they all contain seeds.

You can find the same kinds of fruits growing in the wild, but the wild ones are usually smaller and they rarely taste as nice as the garden ones. The cultivated pears that you can see on the right are much larger than wild pears and they are also sweeter and juicier. Cultivated fruits are nicer because people have been growing them for hundreds of years and have always picked out the best ones to provide seed for the next generation. Plant-breeders are still carrying on this process of gradual improvement, so we can all look forward to even better fruit in the future.

The wild fruit that grows in the hedgerows attracts thrushes and other birds, who eat the juicy flesh and then spit out the seeds – often a long way away from the parent tree or bush. Exactly the same thing happens with cultivated fruit, and this is how young cherry trees can suddenly spring up in your garden. The gardener and the fruit grower have to use nets and bird-scaring machines to stop the birds from taking their fruit. This is especially important with cherries, currants and other small fruits.

Collect as many different garden fruits as you can and cut them all open so that you can see the seeds inside. The boxes below will show you some of the fruits to look out for. Write down the numbers of seeds that you find in each fruit. Are the seeds always arranged in the same way?

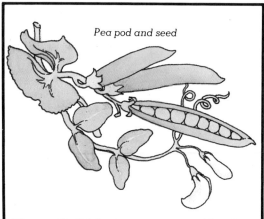

Pea pod and seed

We usually think of **peas** as vegetables, but the pea pod is really a fruit. We generally pick the pods and eat the peas before they are ripe. A ripe pod is dry and brown, and it eventually bursts open and throws out the seeds. **Runner beans** are also pods. Here we eat the unripe pods as well as the seeds.

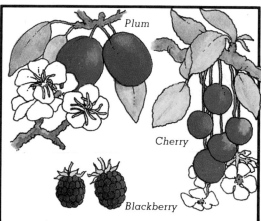

Plum

Cherry

Blackberry

Cherries and **plums** are known as stone fruits. Inside the flesh there is a woody "stone", and the seed is inside this. **Peaches** and **apricots** are also stone fruits. The **blackberry** is really a cluster of little stone fruits: each juicy globule contains a woody pip and seed.

Strawberry

Gooseberry

Red currant

The **strawberry** is not a real berry. Its seeds are inside the little woody pips that you can see on the surface of the fruit. Strawberries grow on low, creeping plants. You can often find them growing wild in the woods and hedgerows: they are small but very sweet.

Lots of small, soft fruits are called berries, but a real berry is a juicy fruit with lots of seeds. The seeds are generally attached to the centre of the fruit. The **red currants** and **gooseberries** shown here are real berries. The **tomato** is also a berry. Can you think of any others?

21

Dancing butterflies

Next time you see some butterflies dancing from flower to flower in your garden, try to get a close look at one of them. See how it pushes its hair-like tongue into each flower. The tongue is hollow and acts like a drinking straw, sucking nectar from the flowers. When not in use, the butterfly keeps this long, long tongue curled up underneath its tiny head.

Several different kinds of butterflies visit the garden to feed, but not many can breed there unless there are lots of weeds and long grasses. Butterflies spend the early part of their lives as leaf-eating caterpillars, and the caterpillars don't like many of our cultivated plants. Indeed, the caterpillars of some of our prettiest butterflies feed on stinging nettles!

One of the commonest butterflies that you might find breeding in your garden is the large white which you can see in the big picture. These large whites are attractive butterflies, but their caterpillars unfortunately eat cabbages. That is why these butterflies are commonly known as cabbage whites.

nature project

The changing caterpillar

Before a caterpillar can turn into a butterfly, it has to pass through a stage called the *chrysalis*. You can see the chrysalis of the large white by the butterfly's eggs at the right of the big picture. It is fixed to a plant or a fence by a silken belt. You can watch the change from caterpillar to chrysalis by collecting some big caterpillars from your cabbages and putting them in a cardboard box. Make sure they always have fresh leaves to eat. You can give them nasturtium leaves instead of cabbage – they contain the same hot-tasting juices as cabbage leaves. Use a sheet of polythene punched with a few small holes as a lid for your box. The chrysalises will soon be formed on the sides of the box. Try putting some of your caterpillars in a green-painted box and some in a yellow-painted box. You can see

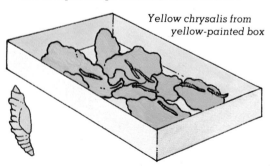

Yellow chrysalis from yellow-painted box

How many butterflies?

How many different kinds of butterfly can you find in your garden in a year? Write down the date in your *Nature Notebook* when you first see each one. Which kind appears first?

The **green-veined white** *(right)* has thick green veins on the underside of its wings. It is a cousin of the cabbage whites, but its caterpillars rarely eat cabbages.

The **wall butterfly** *(left)* likes to bask on sunny rocks and walls. Its caterpillar feeds on grass.

The **red admiral** *(right)* is most common in autumn. It loves to feed on ripe fruit as well as nectar.

from the drawings below that the chrysalises from each box will be different colours. They'll be a similar colour to their surroundings because, in the wild, this helps hide them from their enemies. Chrysalises formed in autumn will not produce butterflies until spring.

Green chrysalis from green-painted box

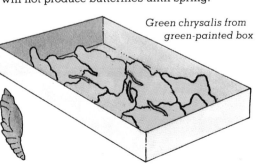

The **peacock** *(left)* flies in late summer and autumn, sleeps all winter and flies again in spring.

The **small tortoiseshell** *(right)* also sleeps through the winter. Like the peacock and the admiral, it feeds on nettles as a caterpillar.

A flock of starlings

You won't have any difficulty in recognising starlings when they visit your garden. They are bigger than most garden birds and they waddle over the ground instead of hopping like most of their feathered relatives. Starlings look black from a distance, but if you get close to them you will see that they have beautiful glossy feathers with a green or purple sheen. The pale spots are more obvious in the winter, when the beak is also black.

Starlings are probably the world's commonest birds. They enjoy each other's company and usually visit the garden in groups, especially in the winter. At this time of year the birds sleep together in huge flocks. You can often watch the preparations for this mass sleep-in from your kitchen window. Early in the afternoon the birds start to gather in the trees. All the starlings from your neighbourhood will gradually join together in one large tree or on a building and make a lot of noise. Then, in the middle of the afternoon, they will fly away together to their sleeping quarters, known as the *roost*. This may be in a wood or a reed bed, or even on a group of town buildings. Similar groups fly in from all over the surrounding area, until in the end the roost may contain as many as 50,000 starlings. They make a tremendous noise before finally settling down to sleep.

The flocks break up in spring, when the starlings start to nest in holes in trees and buildings, but the birds still roam the gardens in small groups as they look for food. Starlings will eat almost anything, and particularly like lots of soft fruit in the summer. You can see a parent bird feeding its brown baby a juicy raspberry in the big picture.

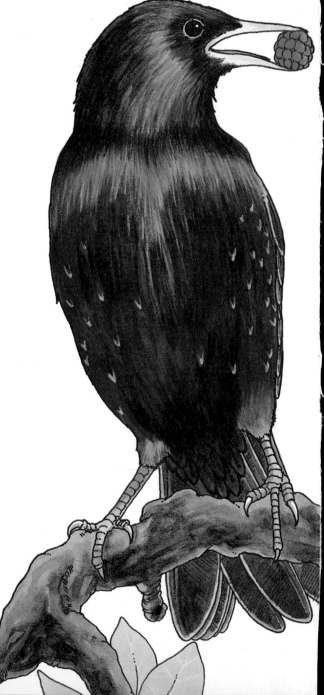

The starling roost

Starlings roost in the same place every night and may fly as far as 20 miles to reach it. If you see a flock in flight in the afternoon, try to mark its flight path on a map. You could do the same thing on another afternoon a few miles away – or perhaps a friend in a nearby village can do it for you. The starlings' roost will probably be close to where the two flight paths meet. Ask someone to take you there to look for it.

Spot the jackdaw

Jackdaws often feed with starlings in gardens and in town parks. They look similar from a distance but you should be able to recognise them by their greyish necks. They are also much bigger than starlings. Both birds dig their beaks into the turf searching for worms and insect grubs.

The troublesome greenfly

You have probably heard gardeners complaining about greenfly on their roses and other plants. These greenfly are small, pear-shaped insects that belong to a large group known as *aphids*. They cluster on certain plants and suck out the sap with their tiny hollow beaks. This weakens the plants, but the insects do even more harm by carrying diseases which can kill our flowers and crops.

The greenfly that live on roses can be green or purply-pink and they are most common in the spring. Instead of laying eggs, like most other insects, they give birth to active babies. Each greenfly may have several babies in just one day and these soon grow up and start to have babies themselves. So within only a short period of time dense clusters of these pests can build up on the plants. Greenfly born early in the year are wingless, but the later ones nearly all have wings and fly off to other plants for the summer. Some of the aphids return to the roses in the autumn and lay eggs on the stems. These eggs hatch in the spring and so the cycle starts all over again.

There are many other kinds of aphid, apart from the greenfly, and between them they feed on nearly every sort of plant. One of the best known and most hated in the garden is the blackfly, which infests beans and spinach. Look at these insects with a magnifying glass and see if you can spot their tiny beaks sticking into the plant stems.

Greenfly and other aphids spend nearly all their time drinking plant sap, which is a sugary liquid. Much of this passes straight through the aphid's body and comes out in the form of *honeydew*. Ants love this sweet liquid and they can often be seen crawling over the aphids and lapping it up. Sometimes they even stroke the aphids to encourage them to give out more honeydew. If you use your magnifying glass and are very patient you may be able to watch them doing this.

The greenfly's enemies

nature watch

Luckily for us, the greenfly has many enemies that help to keep its numbers down.

Look for greenfly on your roses or under red currant leaves and you will probably see one or more **ladybirds**. If not, find a ladybird somewhere else and put it amongst the greenfly. It will soon start to eat them up, as will its bluish-grey grub.

The beautiful green **lacewing** also eats lots of greenfly, and so does its spiky grub. Look for this grub on your plants and watch it attack the greenfly. It sucks them dry with its long hollow jaws, which are like miniature hypodermic syringes. It may camouflage itself by sticking the empty skins on its spiky body. Many lacewings come into our houses in the autumn and go to sleep in odd corners until the warmer weather arrives.

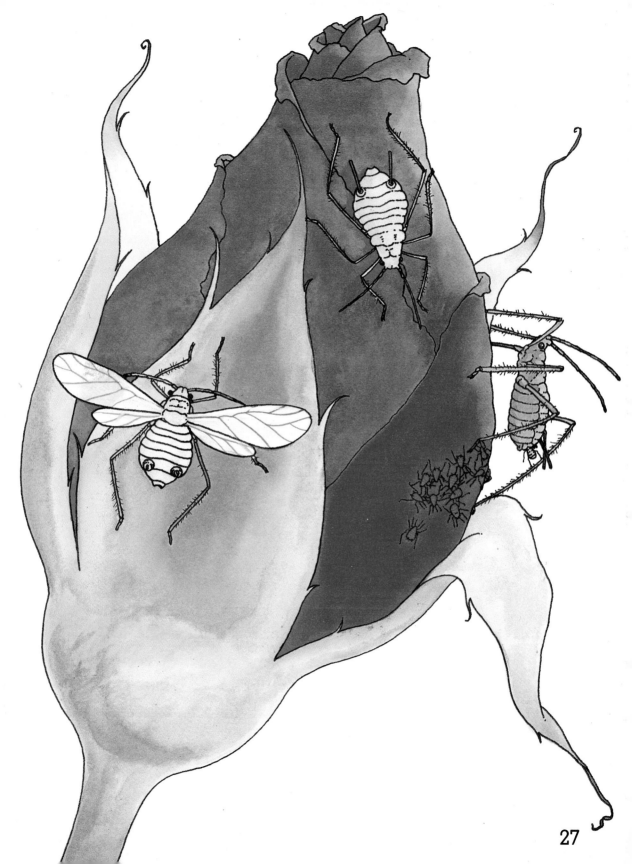

Summer visitors

The bird feeding its babies in the big picture is called a house martin. It weighs only a few grammes and is no bigger than your hand, but nevertheless it flies more than 3,000 miles every year to nest on our houses in the spring and summer. In fact, the house martin comes all the way from Africa, where it spends the winter. It cannot survive the winter in Europe because it is too cold and there is not enough insect food around to keep it alive.

When the house martin arrives in the spring it starts to collect mud to make its nest. It usually builds this under the eaves of a house and, very often, it will return to the nest it used the previous year. If you look carefully at the bird's leg in the picture you will see it is surrounded by a small metal ring. Specially trained bird-watchers are allowed to catch birds and put these rings on them before they let them go. Each ring has a number, and by looking at these numbers the bird-watchers can tell for certain that the martins really do come back to the same houses to nest each year.

House martins catch their food in mid-air by scooping up tiny insects in their wide-open beaks. You can watch them swooping to and fro in the sky, over your garden, catching thousands of flies to take back to their babies.

The swallows on the right of the picture are cousins of the house martin. They live a similar sort of life, but they build their nests on ledges in barns and other buildings rather than under the eaves. Both birds collect on telephone wires in the autumn before starting their long journey back to Africa. Can you spot the differences between them?

nature watch

Comings and goings

House martins and swallows usually arrive in Britain early in April, although the exact date depends largely on the weather. Can you think of any other birds that come to us for the summer? One has a very well-known call that everybody listens for in the spring. It is called a cuckoo.

You can keep a diary to record the dates when you first see these summer visitors each year. You can also record the dates of the autumn departures in your diary. Try to find out what birds visit us for the winter.

As well as writing down the dates on which the summer visitors arrive, try to make drawings of the birds and their nests in your diary. House martin and swallow nests are easy to see and to watch but you must always be careful not to disturb the birds themselves. Use your diary to record the date when you first see the babies being fed. They usually poke their heads out of the nest when the parents arrive with food. When do the babies first leave the nest?

Write down in your diary when you see the birds gathering on the telephone wires in autumn. In what direction do they fly when they leave? You will find that they do not all fly off at the same time. The young birds usually leave later than their parents, but they still find their way to Africa eventually.

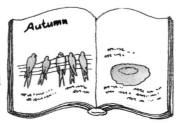

29

Creeping in the dark

As the sun goes down on your garden, the bees and butterflies and most of the birds settle down to sleep. And as they do so, a completely different set of animals comes out to feed. This is the night shift and it includes many of the thin-skinned creatures that can venture out only in the damp night air. They would quickly dry up in the heat of the day.

Take a walk around your garden one night with a torch and see how many animals you can find. A warm summer night is best, especially after rain, but spring and autumn nights can be nearly as good.

Look for earwigs climbing on walls and tree trunks. They eat almost anything and often nibble at insects that have been caught in spider webs. Touch an earwig gently with your finger and watch it try to nip you with its pincers. It won't hurt you, but if you were a small animal trying to eat the earwig, it might pinch your nose hard enough to make you let go. Woodlice also climb walls and tree trunks at night. They nibble mosses and other tiny plants as well as chewing dead leaves. Woodlice are not insects: count their legs and you will see that they have seven pairs, while insects have only three pairs.

The hunting spider in the middle of the big picture is not an insect either: it has four pairs of legs instead of three. This spider does not make a web and it chases woodlice at night.

Slugs and snails crawl all over the garden at night. You can read all about snails on page 14. Slugs behave in much the same way: they are really just snails without shells. Neither of them is very popular with the gardener because they eat many of his plants. Look for signs of

their meal when you're outside.

The devil's coach-horse is a rather fierce beetle with short wing covers. It has large jaws and comes out at night to feed on the other small animals that live in the garden. If you disturb it you will see its jaws open wide, and at the same time it will raise its hind end to try and frighten you away.

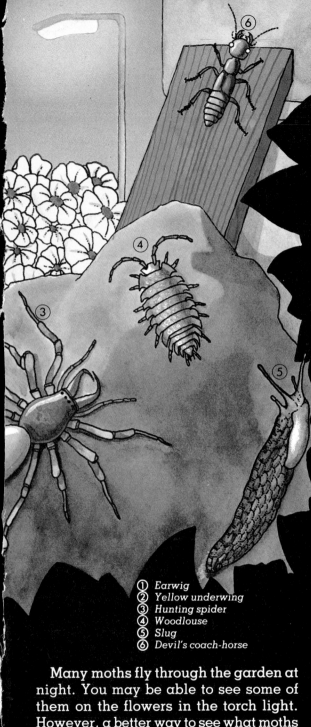

① Earwig
② Yellow underwing
③ Hunting spider
④ Woodlouse
⑤ Slug
⑥ Devil's coach-horse

Many moths fly through the garden at night. You may be able to see some of them on the flowers in the torch light. However, a better way to see what moths are out and about is to shine a reading lamp out of a window. This attracts the moths and many will settle on the window pane. The moth in the big picture is called a yellow underwing.

nature detective

Night-flying moths

Try to identify the moths that come to your window on summer nights. Some of the common ones are shown here. Use a moth book to find out what their caterpillars are like and what they eat.

The **garden tiger moth** *(right)* covers its bright hind wings when resting, but shows them if disturbed. This frightens birds away.

The **swallow-tailed moth** *(left)* gets its name from the short "tails" it has on its hind wings. Its pale colour makes it easy to see in the dark.

The **brimstone moth** *(right)* is one of the commonest moths in country gardens. You may find several on your window.

The **white ermine** *(left)* is a close relative of the garden tiger moth. It has another relative called the buff ermine, which is cream with black spots and dashes.

The **buff-tip moth** *(right)* gets its name from its pale wing-tips. When at rest in the bottom of a hedge, with its wings wrapped tightly round its body, it looks just like a broken twig.

Storing food

Every time you eat vegetables you are really eating up food that the plants have stored for their own use. If we didn't pick and eat these food stores, the plants would use them up themselves to produce their flowers and seeds.

Plants store their food in many different ways. Next time you walk round your garden, or visit the greengrocers, have a good look at all the vegetables and see just how many different parts of a plant we eat. The leaves of cabbages and lettuces are obvious examples, and so are the roots of carrots and parsnips. Can you find any bulbs and stems among the vegetables? We also eat certain kinds of flowers. Can you think of any examples?

Many of what we call vegetables are actually fruits: they do not form until after the plants have flowered. Runner beans are good examples. How many more can you find? The peas and broad beans that we eat are actually seeds. But because the seeds contain food stores to help them to grow into new plants, they are very good for us as well.

What's in the picture?

nature detective

Above are some of the vegetables that you might see in your garden and the parts of each one that you might find on your dinner plate. Can you think of any others?

1 Celery – leaf stalk
2 Lettuce – leaf
3 Pea – seed
4 Onion – bulb
5 Spinach – leaf
6 Parsnip – root
7 Leek – bulb and leaf
8 Potato – tuber
9 Cabbage – leaf
10 Carrot – root
11 Brussels sprout – bud
12 Marrow – fruit
13 Cauliflower – flower
14 Rhubarb – leaf stalk
15 Runner bean – fruit

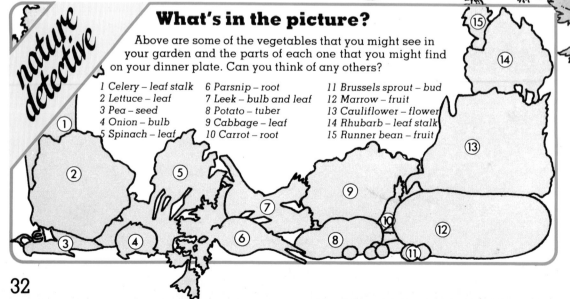

Growing a carrot top

The **carrot** is a biennial plant. That means it takes two years to complete its life. In the first year it stores up food in its root, and if we don't dig it up and eat it, the food is used to produce new leaves, flowers and seeds in the second year. You can watch this food being used if you cut off the top of a carrot and stand it in a saucer of water. In a few days you will see new leaves sprout from the old carrot stump. Their early growth depends on the food stored in the root. However, your carrot will not be able to produce flowers because the small piece of root doesn't contain enough food. You can try this with a parsnip or beetroot as well.

Wasps at work

Many people are afraid of wasps because they can sting. But there is not really any need to fear them: they will not sting you unless you annoy them by waving your arms about. So next time you see some wasps nibbling at a ripe plum or apple, take a close look at them instead of running away. They are really very beautiful insects.

Wasps live in colonies containing several hundred individuals. Most of the wasps that live there are called workers, and they are ruled by a queen, who lays all the eggs. The colony starts life in the spring, when the queen wakes from her winter sleep. She searches for a suitable nesting site and keeps up her strength by taking meals of nectar from the spring flowers. The nest site is usually under the ground, but wasps sometimes hang their nests in the roofs of houses or even in thick bushes. The nest itself is built of paper, which the wasps make by chewing up wood and mixing it with their saliva.

After many journeys to collect and pulp the wood, the queen has enough paper to finish making the first nest cells. These cells have six sides and the queen lays an egg in each one. When the eggs hatch she then has to gather lots of flies and caterpillars to feed the emerging grubs. The grubs soon grow into worker wasps who carry on building the nest and collecting food for new grubs. After this, the queen stays at home and carries on laying eggs.

By the end of the summer the nest may be as big as a football and contain several thousand cells. Some of these cells will contain new queens ready for the next year, but once summer is over the breeding stops altogether. The

workers have no more work to do so they spend their time feasting on the fruits of autumn and – if they get half a chance – anything sweet and sugary that we humans leave lying around. This is the time of year when they can become a nuisance, but they are not around for very long. Only the new queens survive the winter, safely tucked up in a corner, perhaps in your garden shed or loft, ready to start a new nest in the spring.

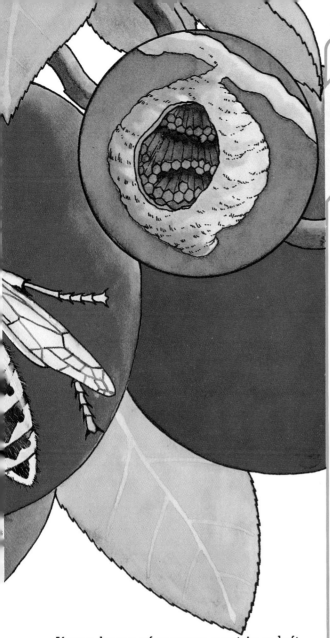

Wasp look-alikes

The wasp's bright yellow and black colouring warns birds that the wasp is harmful. If they get stung, the birds quickly learn to leave black and yellow insects alone. Some harmless insects copy, or mimic, the wasp and they too are left alone by the birds.

Hover-flies are the commonest of the wasp look-alikes. They have no sting and cannot harm you. Look carefully and you will see that the two kinds of hover-fly shown here have only two wings. Wasps have four wings, although the hind wings are small and not easy to see. Hover-flies feed on nectar and pollen.

The **hornet** is a large wasp with a brown and yellow pattern instead of a black and yellow one. It usually nests in hollow trees and often visits gardens. It may raid bee hives to steal honey and to take the bee grubs back to feed to its own young. Although it is much bigger than an ordinary wasp, the hornet is not aggressive and rarely stings people. Even so, you should not disturb it or its nest.

If you know of a wasp nest in a loft, you can safely examine it in the winter to see how all those cells are fitted in. Look also at the fragile, shell-like layers of paper that surround and insulate the nest. You will see from this that the wasp is really a creature to be admired. It destroys lots of the insect pests that are the enemies of the gardener and spends most of its life working on its fantastic home.

Unwanted weeds

If you look in any garden you'll probably find lots of plants that weren't put there by the gardener. They're called *weeds* – plants like dandelions, chickweed and groundsel. And they're not usually very popular with the gardener because they use up the minerals in the soil that would otherwise make his garden flowers and vegetables grow even bigger.

So what *are* weeds? Most of them are simply wild plants growing where we don't want them. But there are two very good reasons why weeds *are* so common in gardens. One is that most weeds produce lots and lots of small seeds that are easily carried into the garden by animals and birds or by the wind. And the other reason is that gardens usually have patches of bare soil where weeds can easily get established once their seeds have landed. They grow very quickly and many are very difficult to get rid of, which is why gardeners are always complaining about them.

The wind carries lots of these small seeds into our gardens, including those of the dandelion which you can see in the big picture. A single dandelion plant can scatter more than 10,000 seeds in a season, each carried away by a little parachute of hairs. Other seeds are so small that they don't need this extra help.

Birds also bring in weed seeds. House sparrows, for example, eat lots of seeds and some pass through their bodies unharmed and all ready to grow where they land. Birds also carry seeds on their muddy feet.

Cleavers or goosegrass has little round fruits clothed with minute hooks. How do you think these fruits are carried into the garden? If you brush your sleeve past such a plant it might give you a clue.

The day's eye

nature watch

Many people think of the little lawn daisy as a weed, but it is still a very pretty flower. Look for daisies on your lawn, in the local park or even on the grass verge at the side of the road. Their name means "the

Weeds from your shoes

nature project

Many weed seeds are brought in to your garden by birds and by the wind, but have you ever thought that you might bring some in yourself? Try this simple experiment after a country walk.

1 It's amazing just how many seeds you can bring home in the mud that collects on your shoes.

2 Scrape the mud from your shoes into a seed tray of potting compost or soil. This should have been baked to kill any seeds already in it.

3 Water the soil well and cover it with a sheet of polythene, or put it in the greenhouse if you have one.

4 Inspect your seed tray every day. It is quite likely that you will find several seedlings sprouting after just a few days. If you leave them to grow they will eventually turn into weeds like the ones below – chickweed, groundsel, shepherd's purse and ... dandelions! You will know for certain that the weeds came from the mud on your shoes because the soil in the tray had been "cooked" to sterilise it.

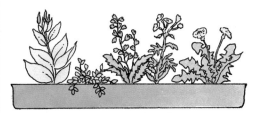

day's eye" because they open with the sun. If you look at your daisies on a sunny day you will see that they are wide open, with their white petals spread out to reveal a bright yellow centre. But if you go out and look at them after dark you will find that most of them have closed up. Can you think of any other flowers that close up at night? Some also close up by day if the weather is cold.

Feed the birds

In the winter, when the ground is frozen or even covered with snow, birds everywhere find it hard to get enough food. You can help them to survive the cold weather, and also give yourself and your family a lot of fun, by putting out food for them every day. The food is best put on a bird table, which you can make very easily from a plank of wood about 60 cms long and 30 cms wide. Fix the table to a post at least 150 cms high, so that cats can't jump on to it. The post should also be thin enough or smooth enough to prevent cats from climbing it.

All kinds of kitchen scraps can be put on the table. Bacon rind, cooked potato, fat, cheese, bread, cake and crushed biscuits are all good for birds, along with apple cores and dried fruit. Peanuts are excellent food, but don't use the salted kind. You may like them, but the salt is bad for the birds. Put the nuts in a string bag and hang it from the table as shown in the picture. You could even get someone to saw a coconut in half and hang the two halves from the table or from a tree. The birds will love the coconut, and when the shells are empty you can fill them with "bird pudding". You can make this from a mixture of dripping, scraps and breakfast cereal – the birds will love it. Remember, though, never to give them desiccated coconut.

To encourage as many different birds as possible into your garden, it is worth buying some special wild bird food which contains lots of different kinds of seeds. You should also put out regular supplies of water when the ground is frozen. And once you have started to feed your birds you must carry on all through the winter, because they will come to depend on you for their food and water.

House sparrow

Blue tit

Which bird is which?

How many kinds of bird visit your garden? Identify them with a bird guide and write their names in your *Nature Notebook*. Try and discover what kind of food each one prefers.

Blackbirds *(above)* are very common in the garden but prefer to feed on the ground rather than on the bird table. Despite its name, the female blackbird is, in fact, brown.

The **dunnock** or **hedge sparrow** *(right)* is a shy bird. It prefers to feed on the ground, but sometimes visits the table.

The **wren** *(left)*, like the dunnock, is a shy little bird. It dislikes open spaces, preferring to stay in the hedge, where it scuttles about like a mouse. Its slender beak shows that it feeds mainly on insects.

The **song thrush** *(right)* has a beautiful voice and often sits high up in a tree to sing its song. Like the blackbird, it is very fond of worms and berries.

Acrobatic bats

If you look into the air above your garden at dusk on a summer evening, you might well see some bats flying at high speed around the trees and houses. Bats are not birds, though, but small furry animals whose wings are really thin sheets of skin stretched over their extremely long fingers. You can see these fingers in the picture. The bats flap their wings very rapidly and make astonishing turns in mid-air. They are chasing moths and other night-flying insects, and they have an amazing way of catching them. In fact, it works even in total darkness.

Although the bat has eyes, they are not very efficient, so the bat uses its ears to help catch its prey instead. As it flies, the bat gives out a stream of very high-pitched sqeaks – far too high for us to hear – which hit objects and then bounce back to the bat as echoes. The bat listens for the echoes with its large ears and can tell the difference between an echo bouncing back from a building and one bouncing back from a moth. These echoes help it to avoid bumping into big objects and at the same time help it to find its high-flying food. This method of finding your way around is called echo-location and the bat can use it to find food even in total darkness. The prey will be caught either in the bat's mouth or in its wing or tail membrane. It may be eaten in flight or carried back to a perch.

Many people are afraid of bats and think that they will get tangled up in their hair when flying overhead. But the bat's echo-location is much too good for this to happen. Bats can even detect telephone wires and avoid flying into them, so it's very unlikely that a bat would ever fly into a human being!

There are many different kinds of bat. The one in the big picture is a horseshoe bat. It is called this because of the folds of skin around its nose and mouth, and if you look closely you will see how they form a horseshoe shape. This horseshoe bat is about to catch a yellow under-wing moth.

Bats fly around for part or all of the night, and sleep by day in hollow trees, caves and buildings. Church towers are favourite sleeping places, and the bats always sleep upside-down with their wings wrapped around their bodies. You can see them to the right of the picture. During the winter, when there aren't many insects to be caught, bats go into a deep sleep called hibernation. They generally choose caves and other well-protected places and enormous numbers of bats may gather to sleep in one place. Never disturb them if you find them sleeping. They are harmless creatures and some species are becoming rare.

Picture index

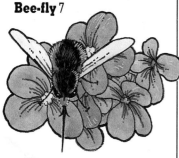
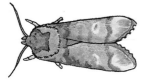

Panel index